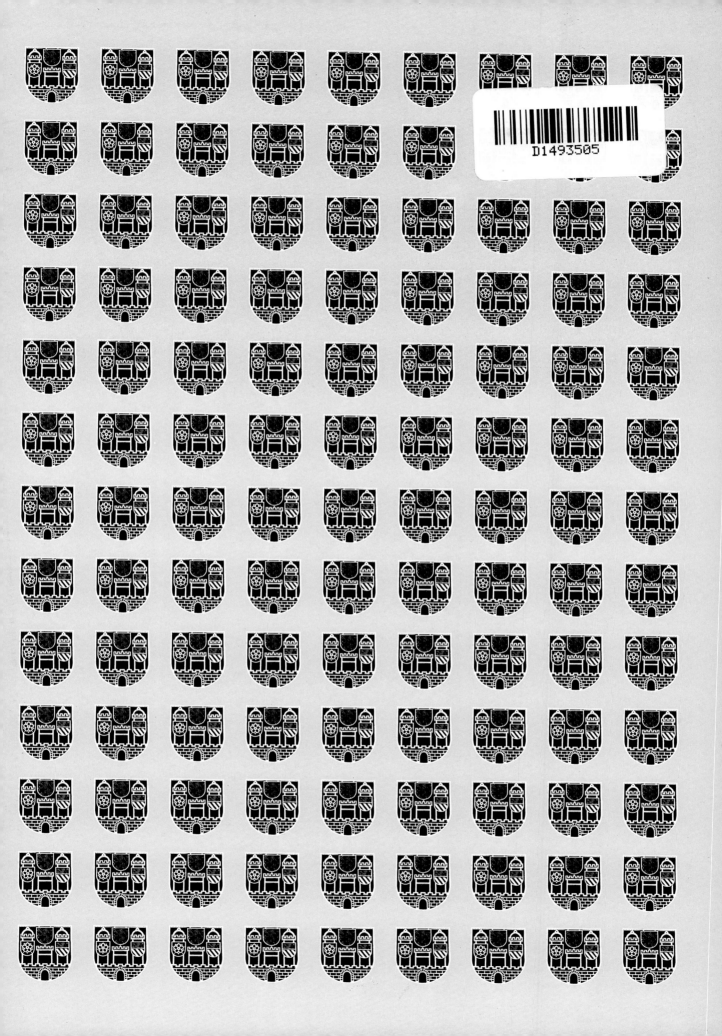

Colditz

FIRST PUBLISHED IN GREAT BRITAIN IN 2001 BY CAXTON EDITIONS
AN IMPRINT OF CAXTON PUBLISHING GROUP
20 BLOOMSBURY STREET, LONDON WC1 3QA

ISBN 1 84067 156 4

A COPY OF THE CIP DATA IS AVAILABLE FROM THE
BRITISH LIBRARY UPON REQUEST

DESIGNED AND PRODUCED BY
KEITH POINTING DESIGN CONSULTANCY

REPROGRAPHICS BY GA GRAPHICS
PRINTED AND BOUND IN
SINGAPORE BY APP PRINTING

ACKNOWLEDGMENTS:
WITH THANKS TO
KENNETH LOCKWOOD, DAVID RAY, THE IMPERIAL WAR MUSEUM, LONDON,
FRAU LIPPMANN AND HERR JOHANNES TSCHECH-LÖFFLER OF THE COLDITZ MUSEUM,

Colditz

A PICTORIAL HISTORY

CAXTON EDITIONS

Colditz Schloss

COLDITZ CASTLE (Schloss) is in Saxony, which although apparently typically German, occupies land originally belonging to Slavs. The Castle dominates the small town of Colditz, 18 miles south-east of Leipzig and was originally built in 1014 as a hunting lodge for the kings of Saxony. It is by the river Mulde, in eastern Germany. During the 15th century it was almost completely destroyed in the Hussite wars. The Castle was later rebuilt as a wedding present for the Danish princess Anne, on her marriage in 1583 to the Kurfuerst of Saxony. They were married for thirty years and had fifteen children. It was she who planted a small vineyard on the slopes across the valley to the north of the castle.

The Castle lay under siege in the 30 years war when the town was allied to the Protestant cause and was sacked in 1634 by the Imperialists. Swedish troops recaptured the castle and occupied it for some years thereafter. In 1706 the Swedes once more occupied the castle in the war with Russia. It later became the official residence of the Dukes of Saxony. The Dukes stopped using

LEFT: The 'White Tower' at the entrance to the castle.
The top of the entrance gate is in the foreground.

it as a residency from 1753 and from 1800 it became a prison. From 1828 some of its dungeons were used to house the insane. It became an early concentration camp in 1933, but was used by the Hitler Youth movement in 1934. At the outbreak of the Second World war, in 1939, it housed Polish Officer prisoners of war and then later Belgian officers. Many of these were released when it was decided that it should be 'special camp' which was to be used mainly for officers who were a high security risk.

Designated in November 1940, as a 'special camp', the first prisoners to arrive were truly international in make-up. They included French, Poles, some of whom had been there before, Belgians, British, Dutch and Serbians.

Those who had been at other POW camps were to claim that the atmosphere at Colditz was unique and like no other. Many of its British Officer inmates had only just left public schools and considered the conditions similar to their old schools. They would buck against authority, throwing paper water bombs at the guards, as they had before against unpopular school teachers.

RIGHT: **Colditz castle, viewed today from the back of the Kommandantur. The windows look east over to the park.**
OVERLEAF: **The castle mid-April, 1974.**

Colditz Town

The Town Hall, situated at the top of the market square, was during the war, where the police were based and weapons were kept. Dating back to the 1500s, the building has itself a colourful history. It was destroyed by fire in 1504 and rebuilt from 1537-40. It was again destroyed by fire after being attacked by the Swedish in the Thirty Years War and was again completely rebuilt in 1657. Today it is used for civil occasions including weddings. The Post Office, located in the town, is like much of Colditz, unchanged in appearance since the Second World War.

ABOVE: The Post Office.
RIGHT: The Town Hall.

Aegidien Kirche

Along with the castle, the church (shown left) dominates the Colditz skyline and all the prisoners would pass it as they entered the castle gates. This Protestant church was first mentioned in 1286. It was rebuilt after a fire in the 15th century.

Belgian Dogs

Before the prison became a special camp, a *Sonderlager*, it was used to house Belgian POWs. On 25 May 1940, a new contingent of Belgian POWs arrived including 96 officers and 12 orderlies and within a few days this had risen to 600 officers and 123 orderlies. Amongst this new intake were six dogs of various breeds. To begin with they were tolerated, despite their barking at night, but it all came to a head when the camp Kommandant, Lt. Col. Schmidt trod into the mess that one of the dogs had made. The dogs were promptly banned and Stabsfeldwebel Gephard (aka 'Mussolini') rounded the dogs up, although attempts were made to hide them, and found homes for them with local dog owners.

OVERLEAF: **An pre-war area view of Colditz Castle and town.**

LEFT: **Aegidien Kirche**

The Bad Boys' Camp

In November 1940, the German Army High Command in Berlin decided that the impregnable looking castle of Colditz should be used as a *Sonderlager*, or a special camp. POW officers, considered to be of high risk status and some VIPs, who arrived in October 1941, were to be kept in one place for maximum security. Strict surveillance was kept on the inmates, as allowed under Article 48 of the Geneva convention. This meant that there were greater searches, more roll-calls and much less room to exercise – only 40 square yards of the prisoners' courtyard. The park outside could be visited for short fixed daily periods but then under some restrictions and under heavy guard. The camp was nicknamed by the Germans as 'Das Camp der Bösen Buben', in English 'The Bad Boys' Camp.'

Hermann Göring after his visit, before it became a 'special camp', declared the castle to be completely escape-proof. However, this proved not to be the case. Being originally built as a fortress to keep people out it was not so impregnable from within, especially when those within held an international array of talent that boasted an expert in almost every field needed to make an escape. There were experts at lock-picking to the making of passes and German uniforms.

The vastness of the place with its disused cellars and empty rooms, enabled the prisoners to work secretly on their many varied escape plans. The ingenious construction of a glider (see page 178) would not have been possible in a more conventional prison-of-war camp. The number of would-be escapees was more than 300, although often these attempts were made time and time again by the same people. In all 130 prisoners succeeded in getting away from the Castle, but most were recaptured before they could leave Germany. Those reaching their homelands numbered only thirty. The French were the most successful with fourteen escapes, followed by the British with nine, the Dutch with six and the Poles with one.

ABOVE: **Field Marshal Göring, head of the Luftwaffe, who claimed Colditz was 'escape-proof.'**

OVERLEAF: **A group of officers and men, POWs in Colditz. Bottom right, right to left Davies-Scourfield, Mike Sinclair, Pemberton-How, J. Watton, D. Bruce. Three orderlies are to the Bruce's left and Scorgie Price is to the far left. Behind Sinclair is Harry Elliott. The men at the back are, right to left: Jimmy Yule, Ralph Holroyd, Bobby Colt, (to his front) Jack Zafouk, Norman Forbes, Teddy Barton, Alan Cheetham.**

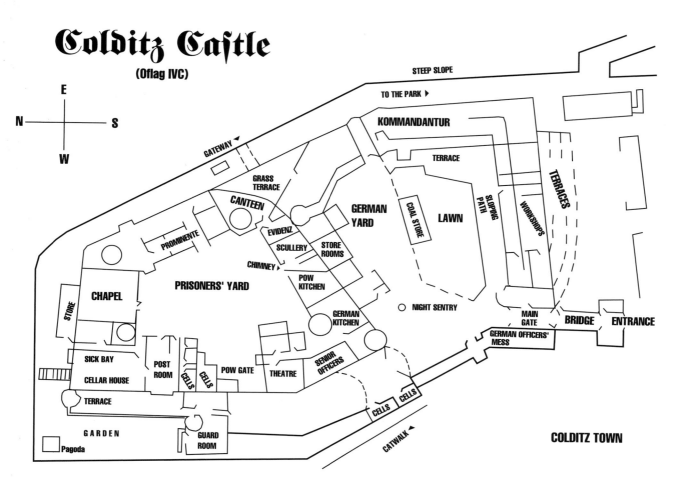

Colditz Castle
(Oflag IVC)

STEEP SLOPE

TO THE PARK ▶

E
N — S
W

KOMMANDANTUR

GATEWAY ▼

TERRACE

GRASS
TERRACE

CANTEEN

GERMAN
YARD

COAL STORE

LAWN

SLOPING PATH

TERRACES

WORKSHOPS

PROMINENTE

EVIDENZ

SCULLERY

STORE
ROOMS

CHIMNEY ▼

POW
KITCHEN

PRISONERS' YARD

○ NIGHT SENTRY

CHAPEL

STORE

GERMAN
KITCHEN

MAIN
GATE

BRIDGE

ENTRANCE

GERMAN OFFICERS'
MESS

SICK BAY

POST
ROOM

CELLS

CELLS

POW GATE

THEATRE

SENIOR
OFFICERS

CELLAR HOUSE

TERRACE

CELLS

CELLS

GARDEN

GUARD
ROOM

CATWALK ◀

COLDITZ TOWN

Pagoda

ABOVE: Map of Colditz Castle as it was during 1940-45.

LEFT: View in the wine cellar, where the French tunnel was built.

LEFT: Entrance to the castle as it was in 1940.

ABOVE: Coat of arms over archway which dates back to the sixteenth century. Airey Neave used the small iron gate set into the right side of the wall leading to the moat, as part of the escape route out of the castle on January 5th, 1942. It was later sealed up for security reasons.

The Guards and the POWs

The guards of Colditz tended to be too old for active service. Reinhold Eggers who wrote *Colditz: The German Story* was over 50 when he first came to Colditz. Others were too young, or had been wounded and were recuperating. While some, such as the unpopular Schädlich, managed to avoid being sent to the front, probably because he owned the hotel/bar in the town, which was frequented by the German officers.

A curious relationship built up between the guards and the POWs, which the German interpreter Herr Hans Pfeifer at Oflag IVC, as Colditz was known, was later to describe to Pat Reid. He explained that it was the prisoners' duty to escape and the guards' duty to prevent the escape. Once someone had managed to escape under such difficult circumstances, it aroused a certain amount of admiration from the Germans, who saw themselves as 'your friend the enemy'.

However, an uneasy relationship lay between the the guards and the Gestapo, recalls Kenneth Lockwood. 'I was in my room with Dick Howe, Gephard (aka 'Mussolini'), and the Gestapo, who were searching my room. One of the Gestapo casually left the some keys unattended. Dick Howe, thinking they would be useful, quickly pinched them. There was an almighty panic from the Gestapo, but Gephard, who must have guessed what had happened, just looked at me and gave me a wink.'

RIGHT: **Even today we can see the discolouration caused by the hasty repair of a tunnel exit, from the Canteen Tunnel Escape.**

First Arrivals

Most new arrivals came via rail and their first experience of Colditz was through this railway station. They were then marched towards the town, across the Adolf Hitler Bridge and up through the market square to the castle. The first prisoners to arrive were 71 Polish POWs and two Ukrainian officers who had travelled for three days in cattle trucks. After arriving at the castle each new arrivals would be de-loused. This was done partly for the Germans' sake who would did not want to catch the lice and was successful as the camp remained louse-free. The de-lousing machine, into which everyone was sent, was so powerful that it would shrink shoes to children's sizes and belts would break like glass.

By Christmas 1940, there were almost 200 prisoners at Colditz – sixty Polish Officers, a dozen Belgian, fifty French and seventeen British plus their orderlies. All had been deemed 'undesirable' by the German authorities. This could be for their politics, anti-German sentiment or, most likely, persistent escape attempts from other camps.

Colditz Oflag IVC was the most heavily guarded POW camp in Germany. One third would be on duty, a third on stand-by and a third off-duty. Apart from during air raids, the Castle was floodlit at night from every angle. The Germans were initially confident that the place was impregnable.

ABOVE AND OVERLEAF: The railway station as it is today. Its appearance has changed little since the war, except it looks a little run-down and the distinctive gothic lettering is missing.

The Bridge to the Castle

The most vulnerable part of the journey, as far as the German Guards were concerned, came after the prisoners had left the railway station. This lay on the western side of the town and so men had to be marched through the street and over Mulde River Bridge, right, as it is today, or the Adolf Hitler Bridge, overleaf, as it was then known, thus giving them a last chance to break for freedom.

The usual pattern was for ten to twenty prisoners to travel together for two to three days on their journey to the castle. Despite being heavily guarded, men did disappear on the way. According to Reinhold Eggers, some would be hastily recaptured such as the Briton, Billie Stephens. A few would disappear for ever, victims without names, perhaps casualties of the war.

The League of Nations

Throughout the war the camp had peoples from most of the allied nations. From 1940-43, there were around 350 British, 14 Canadian, 19 Australian, 10 New Zealanders, 19 Czechs, 1 Maltese, 1 South Africans, 212 Poles, 70 Dutch, 326 French, 36 Belgians, 4 Yugoslavian Serbs, and 1 Indian. From August 1944, 8 Americans eventually arrived. Many of those captured who were from Commonwealth countries were flying for the RAF.

Creatures at Colditz

Colditz had its fair share of flies and fleas. Maggots from the park and dry rot slithers were inserted into the structure of the castle by one long-sighted prisoner, Harry Elliott. He had hoped to bring the building crashing down at some future time.

At one time, large hornets were seen flying around with labels attached on which were written 'Deutschland Kaput.'

PREVIOUS PAGE: Polish POWs marching across the bridge from Colditz in August 1943 as they leave for Spitzberg in Silesia.
RIGHT: The North West corner of the POW yard, as it is today. The courtyard was about 40 yards square bounded on all four sides by the castle building. It was the only exercise space for all the inmates and had a slight slope. On the right is the entrance to the Clock Tower and to its left is the entrance of the sick bay.

Escapes

'Home run' was the term used to describe an escape to a neutral country or friendly territory. There were six made by the Dutch, fourteen by the French and nine by the British. The British made the most escapes from the castle. Many of the French escapes happened from outside the castle. 'Gone away' was the term used for escaping, but later recapture. There were twenty-two British officers who managed to escape, but were later recaptured. Those who completed the 'home runs' were: Airey Neave, along with Dutchman Tony Luteijn, Bill Fowler and Dutchman Van Doorninck, two ERAs, Wally Hammond and Tubby Lister, Brian Paddon, Ronnie Littledale, Billie Stephens, Hank Wardle and Pat Reid. Colditz had the highest number of successful escapes of all the POW camps in Germany. There were eventually about 350 British officers in Colditz and many attempts made, most of which did not come to fruition.

LEFT: **This early picture shows the prisoner's yard. It was encircled by tall buildings which cast deep shadows. A favourite spot to catch the sun was the seat in front of the south-facing chapel. In the corner lies the clock tower, which was to later feature in the major French tunnel escape bid. To the right of the tower, in the top of the attic, the Colditz glider was secretly built.**

The Dutch contingent which numbered sixty by the end of 1942, had about thirty officer-attempts, ten 'gone-aways' and six 'home runs'. The French had one hundred and fifty officers, including fifty Jewish French officers who rarely attempted to escape, as they rightly concluded that they were safer in Colditz than in France. French officer-attempts were twenty to thirty, there were ten 'gone-aways' and four 'home-runs.' The other successful French escapes were from outside the prison walls. Five escaped while being attended to in hospitals, and three while on visit to the dentist.

The Poles who were there from the start, were eighty strong, and were moved to other camps further east later in the war. They had six registered gone-aways, but no 'home-runs', although two escaped from the other camps later in the war.

The Germans, as a matter of course, had a security conference once a week. All new recruits studied the Colditz museum, which security officer Reinhold Eggers started, which documented all of escapes. They were then prepared for the 'tricks of the trade' used by the prisoners.

RIGHT: **View of the Kommandantur building.**

The Kommandants

Schmidt, left, was the first Kommandant from 1939 until 31 July 1942. He was followed by Glaesche, above, who was only in charge from 1 August 1942 until 13 February 1943. Prawitt was last, from 14 February 1943 until the camp was liberated on 16 April 1945 by the Americans.

MI9

MI9 was the British department who was responsible for devising the vast array of ingenious devices which were intended to aid the would-be escaper. As can be seen from the following pages these ranged from the back of a shove-ha'penny board, which contained money, compass and hacksaw blade, to maps hidden in the handles of tennis rackets. Every parcel sent to prisoners was checked. Apparently innocent objects might contain anything from dyes, saws, to identity cards with photographs. Many slipped through and were helpful in prisoner escapes. Those discovered by the parcel inspector became exhibits in the 'Escape Museum'. No contraband was ever sent via Red Cross parcels.

Author Ian Fleming, creator of James Bond, was inspired by the workings of MI9 and based his character 'Q' on people who worked within the department. The late Desmond Llwellyn, who played 'Q' in the films, was himself a POW, but not at Colditz.

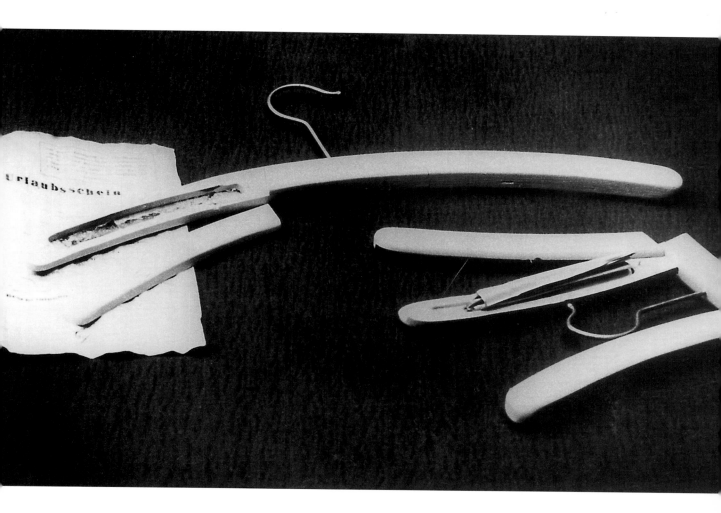

ABOVE: Hidden compartments in coat hangers.

LEFT: Travel bag, with hidden maps.

These apparently innocuous items would have been sent by families, relatives and friends. They were so cunningly hidden that they presented a persistent problem to the Security staff.

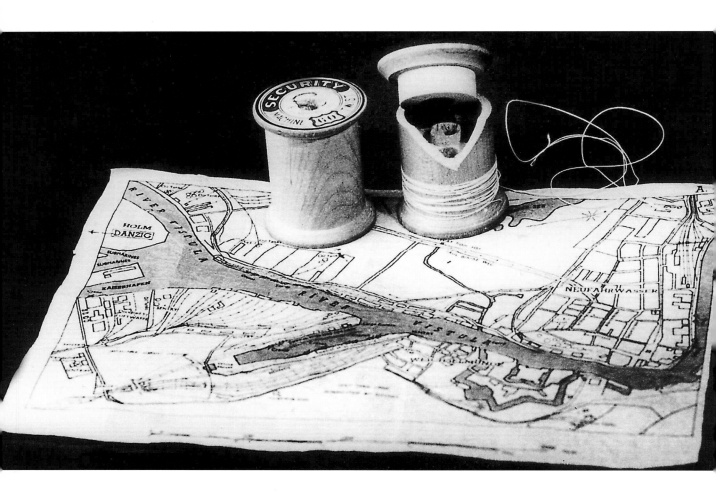

ABOVE: Maps could easily be hidden inside cotton reels. This map shows the river Vistula, leading to the port of Danzig (Gdansk).

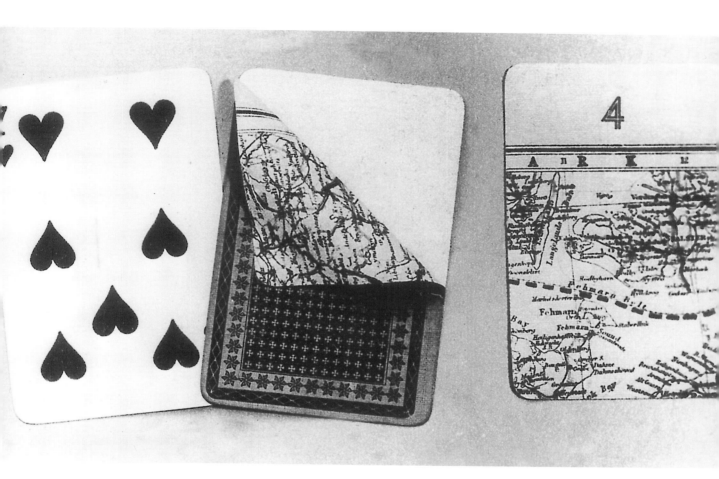

ABOVE: Pack of ordinary looking playing cards reveals a section of a map. When pieced together the prisoner would see a complete map showing possible escape routes.

ABOVE: From a games set, these draughts set pieces contain dyes. These dyes were used for colouring German uniforms, in escape bids.

ABOVE: **A hair brush sent to a French Captain. This had a false top. Inside were found three ampoules and a note signed by a French Doctor stating the Captain had suffered from gall bladder trouble since the age of sixteen. This evidently was the easiest disease to fake and because of this find, the Frenchman's trip to the hospital was cancelled.**

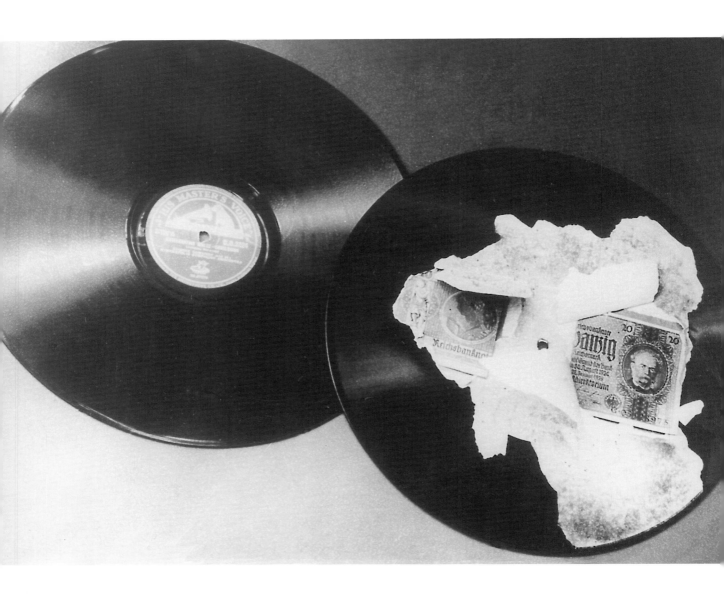

ABOVE: German notes hidden inside a gramophone record.

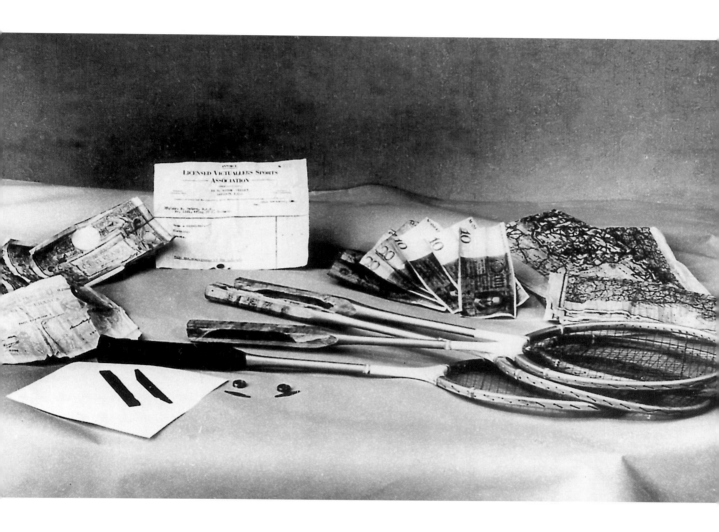

ABOVE: **Money and maps hidden in the badminton racket handles.**

Secret Work

Not only were escape tools sent from outside, they were made by prisoners themselves who were very productive, often working on items day and night. The varied and inventive confiscated escape aids, shown in the following pages, are just a small selection of their work. Their craftsmanship and ingenuity is remarkable.

A speciality of the POW's skills were the keys that they copied. They were so precise that even the Zeiss Ikon security locks became useless. Often the Germans found rooms they believed to be safely locked, stripped bare of all potential escape material. Iron bedsteads, door hooks and many other items were taken and 'converted' into crowbars, stone drills and other heavy tools. Saws were made from canteen knives, pocket knives or razor blades.

Another achievement of the prisoners was the production of forged papers. Much of the paperwork had to be done by hand and in gothic German script. Luitenant Herman Donkers, of the Royal Netherlands Indies Army, became most accomplished in this field. He, like many others, suffered irreparable damage to his eyes because of the strain of such close work. The nibs, taken from the canteen for legitimate letter writing, were filed down to an angle to give the a narrow and broad script. There was even a typewriter, made of wood, to copy official documents, and a camera to take photographs for forged work permits. The typewriter ribbon and camera film were both acquired by bribery.

ABOVE: The Dutch Officers were the best at making bogus German uniforms. Officers' belts and pistol holders were made from linoleum and the Officers' peaked cap, as shown above, were either modified from Dutch ones or made from paper. Cap badges would be cast from plastics moulds, the lead being stolen from water pipes and old telephone cable. The cap braid was plaited from string and coloured in bronze. Seen at twilight these forgeries could fool the most vigilant sentry. BELOW: Rubber stamps used on forged official documents, cut from linoleum.

Whilst digging the tunnels, the prisoner lit them either by installing electric cabling or using their 'home-made' fat or oil lamps. An example is shown above. The tunnel walls were safe as they were well-shored with stolen wooden planks.

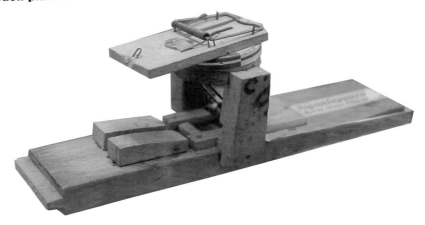

The device above was a mouse trap alert. It was used when the French were digging their tunnel. Every time a German guard was near enough to hear digging or scraping below, the mouse trap was to snap and alert those working below to halt. It was very effective as although the German were suspicious, the French continued tunnelling for about 7 months before discovery.

ABOVE: A wooden sewing machine, made by John Hamilton-Baillie of the Royal Engineers. The German authorities had agreed to its construction so that stage costumes and scenery could be made. However behind the scenes, bogus German uniforms and civilian clothing were being produced with all the efficiency akin to factory mass production.

ABOVE: This hand-made compass was relatively easy to make, by repeatedly stoking the points of two needles with a fixed pole magnet. They would be pushed straight through both sides of the tip of a press-stud to balance each other and lastly balanced on another needle for free movement. This would only be of used once the would-be escaper had left the confines of Colditz and was on his way back home.

OPPOSITE: A selection of hand-made tools from top to bottom: a hand drill, a set of files, a drill, a hammer and a saw. The prisoners used their wooden beds to help in many of their escape plans. They were made into timber roofs in a tunnel, carved into dummy pistols, German bayonets, fake doors and cupboards.

The Outside World

Prisoners were kept in contact with the outside world and the progress of the war via an illegal radio. This was located in the attic above the French quarters. The entrance to the attic, which was out of bounds to prisoners, was through a locked door adjoining the clock tower. However, locked doors did not present too much of a challenge, as prisoners had a stock of home-made keys. The radio had been installed in parts smuggled into Colditz and was for receiving and not transmitting.

The radio cabin created by Lieut. Guigues and his French team was quite a masterpiece. Every contingency had been considered, such as using an alternative power supply necessary when the German had blackouts during air raids to using 'stooging lights' which would flash to warn of danger. German patrols, suspicious of prisoners' outside knowledge, carried sensitive detection devices in the hope of pinpointing the receiver and its location. There was also an escape hatch under the seat of the operator and shorthand writer, so that they and the radio could be hidden. When the French contingent were moved to Lubeck from Colditz they handed over the radio installation to the British. It wasn't until January 1992, when the roof needed repairing that the radio room was finally found.

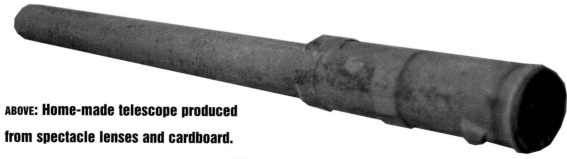

ABOVE: Home-made telescope produced from spectacle lenses and cardboard.

Out of Colditz in 46 days

French officer, Lieutenant Alain Le Ray, right, photographed following his capture in 1940. He was first imprisoned in a POW camp in Pomerania, from which he escaped. After recapture he was imprisoned in Colditz. When he arrived on 24th February 1941, there were 23 French, 80 Poles, 20 British and a small contingent of Jewish POWs. He managed to manufacture a civilian suit and so disguise himself as a German traveller after escaping during a park walk on 11 April 1941. He had noticed whilst taking his regular sorties outside the castle that the park was not particularly well guarded. Judging this day in April to be the right one, Le Ray waited until the column of prisoner rounded a curve in the path, placing a blind spot between the guards and himself, and then leapt up a small embankment and hid in the cellar of the Terrace House until it was safe to scale the park's wall a little later. Under his uniform was the suit he had made. He had worn a wide Khaki coat to cover a small parcel of provisions and the camp doctor placed a 'creeper', a small tube filled with money, in his alimentary canal.

He managed to escape via a train to Nuremberg and from there to the Switzerland, having first mugged a German civilian in order to obtain his coat and money. This was the first successful escape from the Castle and after this Le Ray continued the war as a member of the Resistance and retired as General de Corps in 1968.

Water Bombs and Snowballs

The prisoners made water bombs out of newspapers folded into cocked hats, which they would try and drop onto the guards. When they fell, they sprang open, splashing the target. The cold winters brought snow and the inevitable snowballs. This was not always harmless fun as Reinhold Eggers recalled: one very large ball which narrowly missed him, contained a piece of bottle glass.

Discipline

When a German officer said 'attention', the failure to stand to attention and salute meant, in theory, punishment by five days solitary confinement. But it was only the German Doctor Raum who insisted on such protocol and the threat of this 'punishment' was not so bad as often it was warmer in these cells. Occasionally POWs even requested time away to 'get away from it all'.

Whilst in Colditz all the nations had 'Protecting Powers' to look after their interests. The British had the Swiss, the Dutch had the Swedish, the French had their Scapini Committee and the Pétain Government. The Poles had no nation to protect them, as according to the Germans, their country ceased to exist. Sometimes they would ask the British to act as an intermediary.

LEFT: **Solitary confinement window.**

As the Castle began to fill up, the various national contingents had a different approach to military discipline. The Dutch, several of whom came from the East Indies, were considered by the Germans to be always well behaved on parade, kept their quarters tidy and appeared model prisoners. The Poles were similarly behaved, but the British and French, as way of expressing open rebellion, would not shave and wore pyjamas on parade. The only time the British would be correctly dressed was for the King's birthday.

The Americans

In August 1944, American prisoners started to arrive at Colditz. Colonel Florimond Duke of the US Army was taken prisoner in Hungary, having been parachuted into the country on a special mission. He was captured by the Gestapo, and arrived at Colditz, along with Captain Suarez of the US Army Engineers, Captain Nunn and Major Sabadosh. These were later joined in December 1944, by Colonel Schaefer, US Army, who was kept in solitary under sentence of death. Appeals were continuously being made on his behalf right up to the castle's liberation. No Americans escaped.

RIGHT: **View from the West Terrace to the German Guard house.**

The Bed-Sheet Rope Escape

In May 1941 two Polish Officers, Lieutenants 'Miki' Surmanowicz and Mietek Chmiel, were serving solitary confinement in the courtyard punishment cells. Each cell, bordered on to a corridor and at the end of this was the main door to the yard steps. All doors were kept locked and bolted day and night.

However, late one night, working to a pre-arranged plan, Surmanowicz got out of his cell, released Chmiel from his and then opening the door to the yard, crept out to the courtyard. Once there, their Polish comrades watching from a window high above, quickly lowered a rope made of bed sheets and each officer was hoisted to a ledge. This was forty feet above the ground. Cautiously, keeping a tight hold of the rope, they sidled along the ledge to a gutter, and got up onto the sloping roof of the guardhouse. Climbing up this, with the rope behind, they dropped through a window into an empty attic. They then hung the rope out of the front window which was 120 feet from the

The picture opposite shows the rope of bed linen hanging on the west front of the guardhouse after Lieutenants Surmanowicz and Chmiel had been caught in mid-air, sliding past a window.

ground and started the long slide down. Surmanowicz wore rubber soles but unfortunately Chmiel wore heavy nailed boots, and these scraped the wall as he made his way down. A guard heard them and opening a window spotted the two escapees who were caught in mid-air.

At the time the Germans were mystified as to how they had got out of their cells, particularly as they were found locked the next day. Miki had managed to prise off the batten at the bottom of the door and this allowed him to lift the door off its upright hinge-posts. The door was then opened hinged on the padlock. He then replaced the batten and then put the door back on his hinges. He picked the other locks, relocking them as he went on his way.

ABOVE: Some confiscated keys, made by the POWs.

LEFT: The Guard House, as it is today, was the nerve centre of the German security operations.

The Canteen Escape

The date set for the first mass escape from the British Canteen was May 29th 1941. However, a sentry had reported to his superiors that he had been offered a bribe of 700 marks, then about £50, for turning a blind eye whilst on duty. Therefore, the German security guards became aware that a tunnel escape was to take place but they did not how or where the escape would happen.

The Germans let the digging continue and then on the allotted day, after evening roll-call, lay in wait for the attempted break out. The sentry was to continue to patrol as if nothing was about to happen. As his guard post covered a small lawn beyond the canteen wall, this was the area carefully watched. Hardly believing their eyes, they saw a square turf arising straight from the ground, being held in a wooden frame by four pairs of legs. The frame moved straight up, then out came the head of Captain Pat Reid. Priem, and the others in his party immediately apprehended Reid as other Germans went to arrest those in the canteen.

It appeared that the prisoners had loosened the drain cover in the canteen, and then had made their way along the drain through the side wall. They had picked the locks of two doors so they could dig through the nights. In all, ten British, including the British senior Officer, Colonel German and two Polish officers were caught red-handed. All were in civilian clothing and carried passes. They

RIGHT: **The entrance to the canteen tunnel.**

had 70 marks in real money and a massive haul of provisions – 150lb in weight of Red Cross food, including chocolate, biscuits and tins of food. The prisoners managed to successfully hide the money from the Germans, but a huge haul in provisions was confiscated, as can be seen in picture overleaf.

Thereafter, security measures were tightened up. Sentries were changed at irregular times. Sentries did not return to the same post and so any rhythm in sentry duty, by which escapees could plan their escapes, was broken. The guard who was given his bribe was allowed to keep a 100 marks. He also received extra leave, promotion and the War Service Cross.

The Germans had careful preparations, in case of any future mass breakouts. At Leipzig station some 15 miles away, all the police had duplicate sets of photographs and numbers of all prisoners. All local police stations, foresters and railway stations were also informed. Also mass escapes were not popular always with the prisoners. They rightly worried that if they proved too big an embarrassment to the German authorities then not only were they likely to devote a disproportionate amount of resources to re-capture them, they might also be executed when caught. Fifty were shot after a mass breakout from Stalag Luft III.

RIGHT: Exit tunnel outside the Kommandantur out of which Pat Reid was caught trying to escape.
OVERLEAF: POW food taken from the canteen escape. German security staff including Captain Lange on the right and Captain Teichert, third from the right, pose with their spoils.

Who's that Lady?

Another creative attempt at escape was by Lieutenant Boulé. One day during the prisoners walk back from the park, a middle aged woman tried to walk away from the castle.

'She' was about to leave the castle confines when one prisoner, Squadron leader Paddon, noticed that she had dropped her watch and instead of pocketing it as most would have done, he said 'Hey, Miss, you've dropped your watch!' which she ignored so Paddon passed the watch to a guard, who shouted to the sentry to stop the woman. When the sentry went up to her and looked at her more carefully, he realised that something was very wrong. By the time the guard arrived with the watch, the 'Rhine Maiden' had her fine hat and wig taken off, to reveal the bald head of Lieutenant Boulé, who had been dressed up as woman. When doing the quick change from 'him' to 'her', Boulé had not fastened the watch properly. His plan was almost perfect and had been carefully prepared. His wife had sent him the bronze wig.

However, had the French kept the other nationalities better informed of their escape plans, then Paddon would have just quietly pocketed the watch.

Out in a Box

Flying Officer Bruce was the smallest officer in the British ranks. On 7 September 1942, he managed to squeeze himself into a Red Cross box. German orderlies then unsuspectingly carried him into the store room, from where he broke out and made his escape. Using bed sheeting, he then climbed out of the window, down the outer wall of the German yard buildings overlooking the moat and to freedom.

On the lid of the box he had written 'I don't like the air in Colditz. Auf wiedersehen.'

Unfortunately, he was re-captured at Danzig, and when questioned he said that he had arrived on a stolen bicycle, claiming that he jumped from a British plane over Bremen. However, this story was not believed as his bicycle had a local number on it. He was then sent to the RAF camp at Dulag Luft near Oberursel, where he was recognised by the German staff. So, for a second time he was sent to Colditz. Perhaps he meant to say 'Goodbye' rather than 'Auf wiedersehen.'

RIGHT: View of the clocktower archway, which had the third sentry and second security gate.

OVERLEAF: The empty box out of which Flying Officer Bruce broke free.

Leap-Frog

One amazing escapee was French cavalry lieutenant, Pierre Mairesse-Lebrun, shown on the right as a POW. He had escaped and been re-caught twice before.

In July 1941, he and couple of comrades were leap-frogging by the side of the fence, bidding their time. Then two of them when by the side of an eight foot fence, suddenly clasped their hands together at just below waist level, forming a stirrup, Lebrun ran at them and vaulted over the fence. The sentries immediately started firing but he escaped, although he was dressed only in shorts, a singlet and shoes. He wore a pair of gloves which helped him negotiate the barbed wire. A bullet ricocheted off the wall stinging his face, but he scaled the surrounding wall, as the guard reloaded.

He was able to reach a wheat field some three kilometres from Colditz, walking in backwards and carefully rearranging the sheaves, covering his tracks. Although all the countryside was alerted, they were unable to catch him. By walking and cycling, he reached neutral Switzerland, 400 kilometres away.

Meanwhile he also left a note by his clothes, asking for them to be forwarded to his address in unoccupied France.

The photograph overleaf shows the park wall as is today. Note the plaster on the wall, which was put there by the German authorities to prevent the POWs climbing over.

OFLAG VI B 592

The Long Room Escape

On the last day of July 1941, the Germans foiled a second mass outbreak by the British. This was to have taken place from the so-called Long Room of the British quarters. Knowing that one wall backed on to the wall of the lavatories of the German quarters, the British had begun tunnelling working late at night. However, their assumption that the quarters were empty was untrue. A telephonist on duty and using the lavatory reported hearing scraping noises in the wall to Security. The Germans decided to play a cat and mouse game. Knowing the wall to be only 18 inches thick and that action would take place soon, they lay in wait for the escapees to emerge.

In all ten of the twelve were caught. Here the first out, Lieutenant Peter Allan, re-enacts the event for the Colditz archives.

Madness

Being a POW sent some prisoners a little mad and Francis Flinn, a long term POW and hardened escapee, had an idea. He noticed that prisoners with medical conditions were often repatriated, and decided to 'work his ticket', meaning he would feign madness and try to be sent home. This exhausting enterprise took over a year, before he was taken seriously and sent home as 'mentally ill.'

Recapture

Belgian Leroy and and Frenchman Le Jeune are returned to Colditz on 8th August 1941, under escort, having attempted a daring escape from the exercise grounds.

In order to distract the sentries, their Belgian comrades shouted abuse from their prison windows. They also imitated the sound of gun fire by probably just cracking bedboards together. It was convincing enough for the sentries to fire back in retaliation. Miraculously no one was killed or injured in the shootings.

Meanwhile, the two had cleared the wire fence and were heading towards the park wall. When they could not cross this, they gave themselves up.

LEFT: **Leroy and Le Jeune are taken back into captivity.**

Max and Moritz

'Max' and 'Moritz' were two dummies produced by the Dutch as part of their escape plans. They noticed that at roll-call, the Germans tended to just count the heads of those present, rather than look too closely at facial details. So to conceal the absence of escapees, they decided to make two extra 'people.' Bribing civilian builder nicknamed 'Slam', who carried out repairs at the Castle, they first obtained plaster. Then a Polish officer, who was an accomplished amateur sculptor, cast the heads. They next obtained paints and pastels from Lt. John Watton, of the Border Regiment who held art classes. The heads were placed on frames on which officers hats and coats were placed. The dummies were light enough for officers to carry them in a crowd and without any of the guards being aware.

They were to be part of a plan of escape from the Castle park devised by Captain Machiel van den Henval, nicknamed 'Vandy'. A manhole cover three foot wide had been discovered in the park Gathering around it, while apparently taking part in Bible studies, the Dutch had opened the cover with a spanner they had made out of one of the prisoner's iron beds. They found inside there was enough room to hide two men. The guards were too busy watching a game of football and so were unaware of their important find. Van den Heuvel's idea was to hide two men under the cover during the exercise period covering for them at roll-call times so they were not missed. Later they could make their escape from the park under the cover of darkness.

The first two men to escape, using the manhole, were Captain Rolf Dulfour and Luitenant John Smit on 13 August 1941. Although their absence was successfully covered up by the Germans' carelessness at counting and later by two Poles filling in the missing gaps at evening roll-call, they were recaptured at the Swiss border.

The second attempt was made by Luitenant Hans Larive and Luitenant Franz Steinmetz on 15 August. Just as in the previous attempt, they slipped into the manhole while the attention of the guards was being distracted by a volleyball game. Meanwhile, another Dutchman, Luitenant Gerrit Dames cut a hole in the fence with wirecutters behind his back and at the right moment crept through. When spotted, he shouted 'Run! Run!' giving the impression that others had escaped before him. There was an immediate roll-call and when two men were found missing an extensive search outside the park was made. Of course nobody was found and this left Steinmetz and Larive free to escape that evening and successfully make it to Switzerland, via Tuttlingen in south-west Germany. They were the first Dutch officers to successfully leave Colditz. The third attempt was also successful. This time a Pole and a Frenchman hid under the cloaks and assumed the identity of the missing Poles during the roll-call after returning from the park. Also, as the Germans had bolted the manhole cover after the August escapes, the Dutch made a replacement bolt out of glass. This could withstand inspection

from outside and yet could be broken by the two men, Major Giebel and Luitenant Drijber hiding inside when they pushed up the cover.

It was during the evening roll-call that the ingenious idea of the dummies were put into use. The dummies were either carried by 2nd Luitenant Leo de Hartog (shown here), or 2nd Luitenant Bill Grijzen. Placing them in the centre of the formation they were unnoticed in the half-light, giving the escapees vital time to make their long journey to Switzerland, without being missed.

However, the first dummy dubbed 'Max' by the Germans was discovered three months later on December 12, when it was used again to cover another escape in the park. This time, the guards being suspicious of such a large turn out of prisoners, checked more carefully at roll-call time. They saw the dummy 'Max' close to and in broad daylight so, of course, the game was up. Sniffer dogs were sent to find the missing prisoners Also as the manhole ruse had been discovered and metal clamps reinforced the bolt, the two prisoners were easily found hiding under a camouflaged sheet of leaves. The dummy 'Moritz' was later discovered accidentally in a security search two month later by the No. 1 Security Officer, Reinhold Eggers.

LEFT: 2nd Luitenant Leo de Hartog posing with the dummy 'Max'

LEFT: This picture taken sometime after the escape, shows from left to right; Luitenant Frits Kruimink (whose escape the dummies covered up) Luitenant Diederick van Lynden, Luitenant Gijs van Nimwegen, Max with Luitenant de Hartog, Luitenant Herman Donkers, Luitenant Douw van der Krap and Captain Frits Bijvoet.

FOLLOWING PAGE: Germans hold the net camouflaged with leaves under which two Dutch officers were discovered in the park.

Willy's Brother

Herr Willy Pöhnert was the civilian electrician who worked at Colditz maintaining the electrical installations. Frenchman Lieutenant André Perodeau of the 62nd Regiment of Infantry noticed that there were remarkable physical similarities between himself and the electrician. They were of similar age, hair colouring, height, weight and facial bone structure. The Frenchman carefully studied Willy, noting the style and colour of his clothes and his mannerisms.

Perodeau had arrived at Colditz in July 1941, after successfully escaping from Oflag IVD, by switching roles with a trusted French orderly, one of whose duties included the refuse collection. Perodeau had calmly walked out of the camp whilst carrying rubbish. However, once the alarm was sounded, he was recaptured 50 kilometres away by a German patrol, and was sent to Colditz.

So the idea of impersonation was one that Perodeau was familiar with. After clearing the idea with his superior, General Emil le Brigant, he decided that he should try out his plan just before Christmas when the guards might be less attentive. He managed to tailor clothing exactly to that worn by Willy and also under which have a separate set of civilian clothing. This he could wear

Willy, the camp electrician, right, and his double – Lieutenant Perodeau, left.

once out of the castle. Then he had to forge an identity pass which allowed Willy to enter and leave the Castle. This proved the most difficult part of the plan. The escape committee decided that they could not try to pick Willy's pocket to obtain the pass as although apparently friendly it would be too dangerous to attempt to bribe him. So they waited for a time when they could view the pass, then tried to memorise the overall style of design. An opportunity came, when a French officer had to accompany a guard into Colditz town to collect some Red Cross parcels from the Railway station. He did his best to memorise its design, colour and stamp details when it was presented for inspection. The officer passed all his knowledge back and the forgery experts tried to produce the document. The making of Willy's clothing proved easier. Lieutenant Edgar Duquet, of the 160th Regiment of Artillery, gave his pyjama trousers, which were then dyed. The cap was made out a blanket, and a jacket was made from a bed sheeting and dyed. Bed sheeting was also used to make the yellow swastika arm-band. A Polish officer donated his red woollen scarf, an almost identical version that of Willy's scarf. Once appropriately dressed as Willy, Perodeau tried to perfect his very limited German. This consisted of 'Ich hab's eilig. Ich komme wieder!' (I'm in a hurry. I'll be back later.) He also was to carry maps, Reichsmarks, and Red Cross supplies of figs, biscuits and chocolate, to keep him going for a couple of days. They timed his impersonation to start at just before 5.30 pm one December, exactly when the guards changed and so that Perodeau would not encounter the same shift on his exit. The real Willy was delayed while he was having to attend some minor electrical fault, caused by an little act of sabotage in the French quarters.

Perodeau walked through the first sentry, lit by just a single bulb and he handed the pass which was given only a cursory glance and passed back. He had just three more checks to go. But the second sentry gave the pass a thorough examination and asked him a question, which through his lack German was unable to answer. The sentry repeated the question and receiving no answer pointed his machine gun at Perodeau. He was then taken back to the first sentry, and realising that the plan had failed at least managed to push the map and money under the gate, aware that his compatriots were watching the whole episode. When the real Willy was found on the third floor still working, he was taken and confronted with his double. The only apparent difference was that Perodeau's clothes were cleaner than those that he was wearing. They were both taken to Colonel Schmidt, the Castle Kommandant, who demanded to know how Perodeau had obtained Willy's clothing and whether Willy had knowledge of the

ABOVE: Willy's house in the town, as it is today.

escape plan. Perodeau, who did not wish Willy to be unjustly implicated, explained that Willy was not involved. The Kommandant accepted this, then smiling said to Willy 'It looks as if you have found a new-found brother.'

Perodeau was sentenced to 15 days solitary confinement and never did escape. He was transferred to Lübeck POW camp in July 1943, which was liberated by the British in May 1945.

Meanwhile Willy had to endure teasing for weeks after by the French prisoners, who would shout 'Hey, here comes M'sieur Perodeau!' when they saw him.

After the war Willy and André Perodeau became firm friends, with Willy visiting the Perodeau family in Paris.

Nicknames

All the Guards had nicknames; which they knew of and some even found a little amusing: the policeman was known as 'Hiawatha', his mate was known as 'Minnehaha.' Other names included 'Big Bum', 'Auntie' and 'Fouine', which is French for a ferret, and given to a guard named Schädlich who was clever at finding tunnels. 'Mussolini', was staff sergeant Gephard, who was in charge of the orderlies, and had a reputation for disliking all officers, even his own.

Moral Values

Prisoners of war lived with a strange set of alternative moral values. The Germans once tried to charge a prisoner who had stolen a bicycle. He was acquitted though, because his German defence lawyer said that a German prisoner of war had stolen a vehicle which helped him escape back to Germany. Therefore theft was considered perfectly legitimate. This also meant that prisoners could carry false papers, give false information to police and commit certain other crimes for which the German population would be severely punished, if not even executed.

The worst threat POWs would normally expect upon recapture would be given a maximum of 28 days solitary confinement. They could, however, be shot whilst attempting to escape. This took place particularly later in the war, when the Germans were losing. If an escapee fell into the hands of the Gestapo or SS after 1943, then there was a likelihood of being shot.

OVERLEAF: Dutch Cadet Charlie Linck, has to recreate his attempt to escape in a sack for the Colditz Museum. His bid was thought be foiled by information given by a collaborator.

Collaboration

Collaboration between the POWs and the German authorities was extremely rare. When it did occur, it was likely to be because of veiled threats against family members rather than for any ideological reason. Only one French and Pole were suspected by their compatriots. On one occasion the Germans were informed that unless they removed within 24 hours a French prisoner from the midst of his compatriots, he would come to great harm. He was taken away and was not heard from again. Even today the name of this man is still unknown.

One case of suspected collaboration came when a Dutch officer called Linck tried to escape along with Flight Lieutenant Francis Flinn in a bag in the spring of 1942. They had noticed that Poles were given the task of transporting sacks to a horse drawn cart and the contents were not checked by their German guards. The idea was put to the Poles to place the two escapees, who were both slight, into sacks. The cart would be driven out of the castle grounds and they would have then climbed out of the sacks and escaped. They chose the day and all appeared to go according to plan, except that once the sacks had been placed on the cart, four large German soldiers jumped on the cart and started to kick all the bags, and the two escapees were forced to give themselves up.

When Kommandant Schmidt was informed of the traitor, a man named Bednarski, by the British on behalf of the Poles, he was transferred from Colditz that day. Bednarski later committed suicide in Poland.

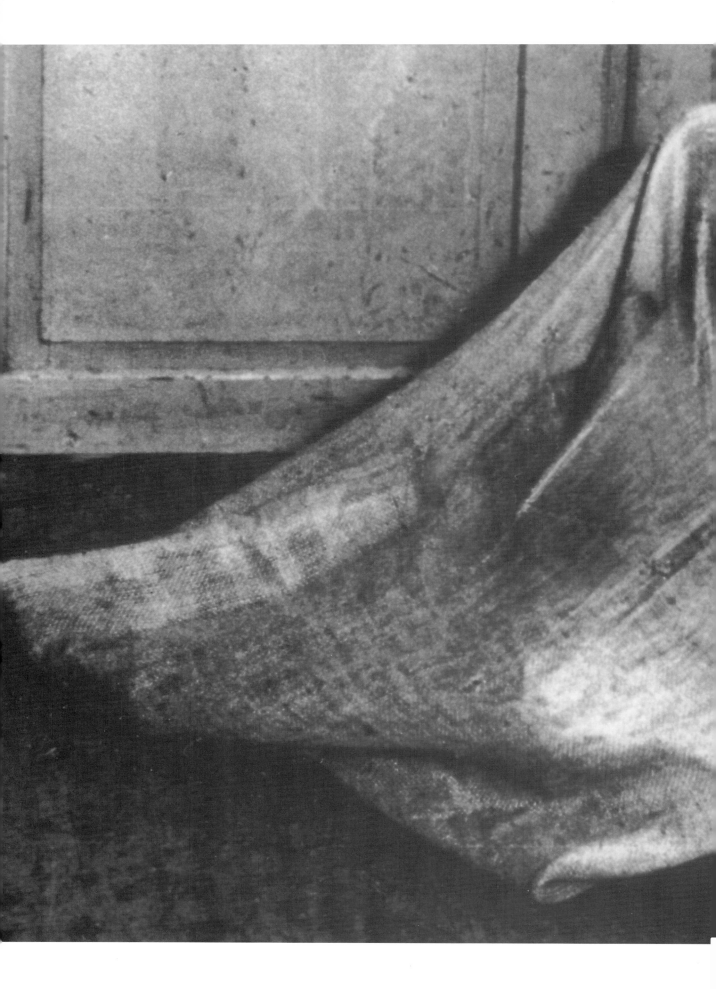

The British Traitor

Walter Purdy, a naval Lieutenant, was before the war a member of Oswald Mosley's British Union of Fascists. An engineer in the merchant navy at the start of the war, he was transferred, along with all other merchant seamen, to the Royal Navy. He was captured by the Germans after his cruiser ship sank off the coast of Norway. He asked to be put into contact with Lord Haw-Haw in Berlin and there he was put in a 'rest camp' along with others who the Germans wished to persuade to fight the Russians under a new force, known as the British Freikorps. He was later to admit that he helped Haw-Haw for eight months.

Purdy then was given the task of being a 'plant' inside Colditz and give information about the series of escapes that had been embarrassing to the German high command. He arrived on 8 March 1944, and managed to report on the activity around one tunnel but his activities were soon curtailed as a Captain Julius Green, who travelled from camp to camp carrying out dental surgery, knew of him and tipped off the British officer in command.

Once the Germans realised that his cover was blown they withdrew Purdy from Colditz on 11 March and after a period in the cells, he went back to his mistress in Berlin until the end of the war. After the war he was sentenced to hang, but was reprieved two days before the date of execution and served nine years in prison. When released, he returned to Britain and married, but never told his wife of his wartime treachery.

The First British Escapee

It was on 8 May 1941, that the first British prisoner, Lieutenant Peter Allan, managed to escape out of Colditz. He, along with Lieutenant John Hyde-Thomson, were each packed into separate palliasses (straw mattresses), on separate carts. Ironically, items of unused furniture and equipment were being removed from the Castle in order to deprive prisoners of raw escape material.

Allan was chosen because apart from being small and light, he also spoke fluent German, having studied at Jena before the war. His colleague, by contrast, was tall and heavy and proved to be a poor choice. The French had difficulty in lifting the other palliasse, with Hyde-Thomson onto the cart. It was left on the ground in panic and his hiding place was soon discovered. A guard organising the transport stepped back and then investigated a large hard lump in the mattress. With his discovery, an alarm was sounded and the carts were checked but Allan was already out of the castle grounds.

It was Allan's excellent German probably saved his life, as when hitching a lift, he was picked up by a senior German SS Officer. Capture by the SS or Gestapo could have resulted in him being shot as a spy. Fortunately, after 50 kilometres, he was dropped off. After ten days, he arrived exhausted at Vienna and and went to see the American Consul. As many of the staff were German and his American accent wasn't so good as his German, they became suspicious. When he confessed to the Americans that he was an escaped British officer and wished to reach Budapest, then a neutral country, the American Consul said 'I am afraid the United States is neutral too. We cannot assist you in any way.' Filled with ever growing despondency, now hungry and without money, Allan was forced to spend the night on a park bench. Because of severe cramp he crawled to the nearest dwelling and was sent to hospital, from where he was returned to Colditz to serve the customary month's solitary confinement.

The French Tunnel

One attempt at mass-escape was the tunnel dug by the French. Starting in roof of the the clock tower, it went through the ceilings of three floors through to the wine cellar, under the chapel and then deep underground towards the steep slopes of the park outside. The tunnel took eight months to build and was a formidable piece of engineering, with even its own lighting under the chapel. It was dug using rudimentary tools on brickwork and rock. Many tunnels were dug in Colditz, but this was the grandest in terms of scale.

It was very near to completion when Gephard and a boy assistant, after many fruitless previous searches, finally discovered its starting place in the clock tower. At that time the French only had another ten feet to dig to reach the outside.

RIGHT: View taken looking down one of the floors in the clock tower.

ABOVE: Inside the chapel. It originally had paintings by Cranach.

RIGHT: Entrance to the chapel as it is today.

OVERLEAF: View, looking up, of the chapel.

Relieving the Boredom

When not planning or attempting escapes many prisoners found themselves very bored. The different nationalities tried to teach each other their languages. Amateur artists gave lessons, stage plays were written and performed. The theatre became an important part of cultural life in the camp. Some plays and shows became relatively sophisticated and included work by Noel Coward, along with others such as 'Ballet Nonsense', shown overleaf.

But like in any prison environment, time passed by slowly and during the winter months some would retire all day to their beds just in order to keep warm.

A poster appeared bearing the following words, which shows with some irony the frustration that most must have felt:

For Sunshine holidays

visit

Sunny Colditz

Holiday Hotel

500 beds, one bath

cuisine by French chef

large staff

always attentive and vigilant

once visited, never left.

Ballet Nonsense

Plays and shows helped prisoners pass the time at Colditz. As it kept them occupied, the Germans allowed the POWs some spare wood and clothing to produce props and theatrical costumes. All the dresses were made out of paper, and scenery and furniture were made out of paper, cardboard and wood. All seats were charged at one mark each and the band would play in the interval.

However, the POWs used every opportunity to aid their many escape attempts.

The photograph overleaf, shows the play 'Ballet Nonsense' performed by the British POWs in 1941. Neave and Luteijn intended to make their escape in the finale, knowing that the Kommandant and his senior officers were to watch the play and that the sentries in the guards quarters would be also more relaxed. However, delays in their escape preparations, meant that this plan was postponed until a later date.

Four of the men shown in this picture did eventually escape: Airey Neave, seen on the left wearing a mortar board, Pat Reid as the Ballet Dancer in the centre, Jacques Prot, the dark haired saxophonist and Luteijn, the Dutch double bass player who escaped with Airey Neave.

Dirty Linen

In the summer of 1942, the POWs had noticed that four Polish orderlies undertook the chore of carrying out two large boxes of dirty German clothing to be cleaned. They were escorted by two German guards and took the boxes to Zschadrass, a village about 3 kilometres away. Here the clothes were washed and ironed and then returned to the castle.

This was seen as an opportunity by the British and Dutch POWs. The path taken by the orderlies was through the castle park, known as the Tiergarten and from here it would easy to escape and disappear. A plan was made to impersonate the two German guards and the four Polish orderlies.

They needed an exit and had an audacious idea. Captain Kenneth Lockwood, feigned sickness and was sent to the sick ward, right next to the Regimental Sergeant Major Gephard (aka 'Mussolini'). Once in the ward, he was able to receive visitors, Pat Reid and Lieutenant Gill. The two man party hid under the bed and at night used keys forged by master locksmith van Doorninck. Once in Gephard's office, they carefully removed the floorboards from under his desk and cut diagonally through into the clothing storehouse. From here the POWs could walk out of the door and onto the park gate posing as the Polish working party.

The operation was completed in only a few days. After each excavation, the nails and even dust, collected in the British quarters were carefully placed over the tunnels entrance. Work was carried out throughout the night and early morning they hid back under Captain Lockwood's bed. Meanwhile Luitenant Donkers was busy producing false identity papers and work permits.

When the uniforms and self assembly boxes were ready they, along with four others, hid quietly until 2am, allowing themselves three hours to complete the operation. Aided by Reid and Gill, to tidy up and keep the plaster intact, they started their journey the following morning. The real test, would be at the security gate, where fortunately the sentry opened the gate without waiting to be asked. They walked straight out into the park and freedom – at least for a time. Four were recaptured, but two made it to Switzerland and home.

OVERLEAF: In this recreation of the escape, real Polish orderlies were made to stand in for the missing escapees: Those missing were: Luitenant Beets, Lieutenant Lawton, Lieutenant Geoff Wardle and Flight Lieutenant Fowler. In the real escape, Luitenant ter Zee van Doorninck, who spoke fluent German played the part of the senior NCO and Luitenant Donkers, a private. Luitenant van Doorninck and Flight Lieutenant Fowler made a 'home run', all the way back to Switzerland after an 87 hour journey.

The Red Fox

Mike Sinclair, of the King's Royal Rifle Corps, was dubbed 'Der Rote Fuchs' (Red Fox) by the Germans because of his hair colour and the wily escape plans. One of his most audacious was when he impersonated the elderly German Sergeant-Major Rothenberger, nicknamed 'Franz Josef' by the POWs. After spending weeks studying the posture mannerisms of his target, making the appropriate costumes and facial disguises, he was ready.

Along with two others, Captain Lance Pope and Lieutenant John Hyde-Thomson who were to be dressed as guards, they planned to relieve the sentries on the gate. Once clear, another 30 prisoners were set to follow in the biggest breakout from Colditz known. The date set was September 2 1943, when a particularly stupid guard was expected to be on duty. They passed the first sentry and then Sinclair slipped up, by missing a particular mannerism of Franz Josef. He made the mistake of not looking both sides of the catwalk before crossing. This was immediately picked up by the guard, who was more astute than he had been given credit for. He asked to see the guard commander's pass which was the wrong colour. He raised the alarm and in the ensuing conflagration, Sinclair was shot in the chest. Although seriously hurt, he was arrested and put into solitary confinement as a punishment.

RIGHT: Stabsfeldwebel Rothenberger, known to the POWs as 'Franz Josef.'

This did not stop Sinclair trying again, making a ninth and fatally, his last attempt at escape. On a mild day, 25 September 1944, Sinclair was walking around the inside of the wire. He suddenly jumped over the trip-wire, reaching the main fence which he climbed over with his thick gloves, gripping the barbed wire. An NCO ordered him to stop and attempted to shoot him but his revolver misfired. Sinclair ran 150 yards down the ravine, where the stream ran through a grid under the foot of the ten-foot wall which surrounded the park. He could not get through the grid nor climb the wall, by which time several sentries had opened fire. A bullet ricocheted off his elbow and pierced his heart, killing him outright. He was just 26 years old.

Within seven months, the castle was liberated, and if he had not made that fateful attempt, he would have been free. But he was doing his duty as he saw it – getting back to England at all costs. He was buried in the military cemetery at Colditz with full honours and later his body was moved to Charlottenburg Commonwealth War Graves Commission Cemetery in the west of Berlin.

LEFT: Lieutenant Michael Sinclair, 'The Red Fox', the greatest escaper of them all, shot and killed whilst attempting to escape.

ABOVE: This is the part of the park where Mike Sinclair was shot dead, as it is today. At the time it would have had barbed wire which he would had to negotiate before he could reach the wall.

RIGHT: Lieutenant Lance Pope of the Royal Fusiliers, who impersonated a German sentry in the 'Franz Josef' bid for escape.

OVERLEAF: The castle viewed from the park, Kommandantur to the left and prisoners' quarters to the right.

Douglas Bader

Wing Commander Douglas Bader was the legendary Battle of Britain fighter pilot who lost his legs in a flying accident before the war. He learnt to walk again, with great bravery and persistence, on artificial aluminium legs and returned to flying planes, shooting down twenty-two of the enemy's aircraft. However, he was shot down near St Omer, France. He escaped with the aid of bed-sheets from hospital and then another two times from prison camps before being sent to Colditz in May 1942. His life was famously celebrated in the film 'Reach for the Sky' starring Kenneth Moore.

Whilst at Colditz the Germans, respecting his courage and notoriety, gave Bader many special privileges. He was allowed one hot bath a week (which he shared with his mess) and he was allowed to go for walks outside in the country so that he could exercise the muscles at the top of his legs. He needed extra strong muscles in order to propel his metal legs when walking. It was while on these walks that, although attended by two guards, he openly traded contents of the Red Cross parcel with the local farmer's barley. This was a much needed bulk food and used for making porridge during the cold winter months. He obviously flaunted all the rules and was the only prisoner to get away with it.

Douglas Bader had a great sense of humour, often making jokes at the German's expense. It was only his disability that stopped him trying to escape from Colditz.

Johannes Lange

Johannes Lange was born in the town of Colditz in 1901, the only son of Moritz Lange, who supplemented his modest income by photographing weddings and christenings. Johannes, under the direction of his father, made a career as a photographer but was interrupted because of the outbreak of the Second World War. At the age of forty he was ordered to serve the Fatherland, not as a soldier but in his capacity of photographer, taking pictures relating to escape attempts at Colditz Castle. As there were so many attempts with such invention and variety, he was kept busy and his pictures were used as a teaching tools for the guards to learn about the clever ingenuity of their prisoners. Many of his pictures are reproduced in this book. These pictures stopped in the autumn of 1943, when negative film became difficult to obtain.

He also took pictures of individual and group of prisoners which were sent home to family and loved ones as proof of survival. On the proceeds, he was able to establish his own photography business after the war which was very successful. He died, a wealthy bachelor, in 1975.

overleaf: Group of British POWs including Douglas Bader. Top, left to right; Best, Forbes, Zafouk, Flinn, van Rood, Halifax, Donaldson, Thom, Milne, Middleton, Goldfinch. Bottom, left to right; Dickinson, Stephenson, Parker, Bader, McCall, Lockett, D.Bruce.

Prominente

Those called Prominente were set apart by the German High Command. They were persons who by birth or fame were thought to be of value. It became obvious to all that, as the war progressed, they would be used by Hitler or Himmler as hostages. They included Giles Romilly, who was Churchill's nephew, Captain the Master of Elphinstone, a nephew of the then Queen (now known as the Queen Mother), Captains the Earl of Hopetoun, Michael Alexander, and Earl Haig. They were allowed to mix with others prisoners but had their own roll-call, special guards and their own cells and were not allowed in the park. Towards the end of the war there were seven or eight British Prominente in number. General Bor-Komorowski, leader of the Warsaw uprising and his staff, made the total up to twenty.

Giles Romilly

Giles Romilly was a political prisoner having been captured in Narvik, Norway in April 1940 whilst working as a *Daily Express* reporter. Interned in Bavaria, he escaped disguised as a woman and was recaptured. Regarded by Hitler as a 'Prominente', a special prisoner, as he could be such a valuable hostage, he was sent to Colditz on the 25 October 1941, by order of the German High Command and placed under special guard. The Germans gave him the cover name of 'Emil.' A spy hole was put on his cell door, blue electric light was always turned on and his presence was checked regularly day and night. He was also not allowed to take part in park walks.

He did, however, make two attempts to escape, firstly by unsuccessfully disguising himself as a Polish orderly and then later hiding in a box with luggage that was to be taken out of the castle. Unfortunately for Romilly, it was a hot day and the hole drilled in his box was small. He was caught removing the lid in order to get some air. Had he escaped, the Kommandant would have received the death penalty, for such was the value placed on him as a prisoner.

He, along with other Prominente hostage prisoners were removed from Colditz on the evening of Friday 13 April 1945, just before the castle was liberated on the morning of the 16 April. In the end they were not used in a hostage exchange as there was total confusion in South Germany as the end of the war approached. When they were moved to a castle at Tittmoning, Romilly escaped with the Dutchman, Luitenant Tielman and succeeded in rejoining the Allies in Munich. Here, with the other Prominente, they reached the American lines without being hurt.

OPPOSITE: **A reconstruction of Giles Romilly's cell, showing his bed.**

OVERLEAF: **The view from his cell.**

Escape from the Dentist

On December 17 1941, a dentist's visit became a golden opportunity for escape. As their French officer dentist had only the material for simply fillings, a party of seven men were sent to the town dentist with a guard. After treatment, three French officers took advantage of the foggy, wet conditions and disappeared into the night. The guard was in a hopeless position as he could not run in three different directions, nor could he fire blindly into the thick fog. Lieutenants Durand-Hornus, de Frondeville and Trot all successfully made it back to France.

Chateau Colditz

Captain Michael Farr attempted to escape from several prison camps and had been recaptured on numerous occasions. Eventually he was, like many others, sent to Colditz.

Finding that escape from this formidable fortress was not so easy, he put his spare time to use by the study of winemaking. With help from fellow French prisoners and books on wines sent by his mother, he evolved a simple recipe. This consisted of putting dried fruits, such as apricots, prunes, sultanas and raisins into a gallon jar of water. This was then put down behind one of the large stoves in Colditz, so that an even temperature could be maintained during the fermentation period. They had been able to get a small amount of yeast and were able to keep this alive during the winemaking. It took four to six weeks for the sugar in the wine to turn into alcohol. After discovery, the wine was at first confiscated but in the end Captain Eggers allowed the brewing to continue.

Michael Farr went on the produce a rose wine and sparkling wine which the men named 'Farsac' and 'Champenoise' for a joke. He also made a spirit somewhat like Schnapps which was very potent. After the war he joined an old family business of wine merchants.

Mealtimes

Mealtimes were tedious to say the least, so parcels from the Red Cross were most welcome. There were bulk parcels, not individually addressed and were dispatched at the rate of one per week per person, sometimes more. Smaller parcels also arrived from the United Kingdom, Canada and later from Australia, New Zealand and the USA. Food included tinned meat, vegetables, cheese, jam and butter, powdered egg, powdered milk, tea or cocoa, chocolate, sugar, and cooking fat and were all greatly appreciated. Not all parcels contained food. Cigarettes, clothes, books and gramophones records also arrived for inmates, although as can be seen, these often contained ingenious artifacts for escaping. In addition, private parcels could be sent to each prisoner four times a year.

The French received food parcels mainly tinned meat which came from Madagascar and large quantities of French army biscuits called 'Biscuit Pétain' which they traded with the British for cigarettes. They also had a reputation for their flair in using mundane and limited ingredients to create mouth-watering meals. On one such occasion a main course prepared for some British officers led to much praise. 'Was is rabbit?' they enquired. To their amazement the cook admitted that they had just eaten the pet cat belonging to one of the officers!

Rations

As the war progressed, rations deteriorated. Below is a typical example of a meal on offer.

Monday to Friday (a small portion of cheese was added on Fridays)

Breakfast	Lunch	Dinner
Coffee-substitute 4gr	*Potatoes 400gr*	*Jam Substitute 20gr*
	Turnips 500-600gr	*Bread 300gr*

Weekends were slightly better. On Saturday, millet, oats and barley were added to meals and Sunday was like any other weekday, but 250grams of fresh meat were allowed at lunchtime.

OVERLEAF: **German Christmas celebration dinner at Colditz, 1943. On the far left is Captain Eggers, author of 'Colditz: The German Story', published in 1961.**

Reinhold Eggers

Before the war, Eggers was a schoolteacher, with hopes of becoming a School Inspector until he was denounced by his colleagues and demoted for being anti-Nazi. In 1940, aged fifty, he was called up by the army and transferred to the POW service, as he had an excellent command of both English and French.

He was the longest serving member of the Colditz security staff arriving in November 1940, and stayed there until its liberation. For the last fourteen months he served as Chief Security Officer, accumulating a vast amount of historical material which he managed to keep after the war was over.

In 1946 he was imprisoned by the Russians who were the occupying power in his home town of Halle and served ten years hard labour. After his release he published in 1961, *Colditz: The German Story*, which told the Colditz story from the guards' perspective. He died in 1974.

RIGHT: Reinhold Eggers, the camp officer at Colditz until February 1944, when he became Security Officer. This photographs shows him wearing the Iron Cross from World War One.

Contact with the Outside

The Czech flight lieutenant, Cenek Cheloupka, called 'Checko' at Colditz managed to get a girlfriend from the village. He had met Irmgard Wernicke on a train, when he had been travelling to Prague for interrogation by the Gestapo. Being tall, handsome and charismatic in character she soon became infatuated with this young officer, waiting for every train returning from Prague in hope of seeing him once again.

As luck would have it, she worked as a dentist assistant at the Castle. Checko managed to get to the dentist, it has been said, by damaging his front teeth. Each time he attended for treatment, he was able to see Irmgard on her own. She had great sympathy for the POWs, was anti-Nazi and very willing to help. He passed letters to her so she could mail them to a friend in Switzerland who then remailed them to England.

When his treatment was completed, a young guard was found to act as a courier. He carried what he thought were love letters to Irma. These were in fact reports on conditions in the area and letters informing the allies command of troop activities. The prisoners kept abreast of military developments by German newspapers, given to them by the authorities and unknown to the Germans, received the BBC news. Also as Irma's father was the director of an agricultural school, he had many visits from Nazi officials. This connection enabled her to pass invaluable information on to the prisoners.

After the war when the Soviet army occupied Colditz, Irma decided to leave when the secret police came looking for her. She disliked Communists as well as Nazis. Meeting another freedom fighter, she married and after an adventurous life, settled in Castaic, California.

Colditz Ghosts

Two Dutch officers, Flight Luitenant Van Rood and Captain Dufour, were discovered trying to escape dressed as German officers. With their forged identity established, the sentry had saluted and made way to open the gate. However, as they made their exit, Dufour smiled and waved to the guards, one of whom recognised his gold tooth.

Their capture prompted a roll-call and it was found that two men were missing. These were Lieutenant Michael Harvey, RN, and Flight-Lieutenant Jack Best, RAF. It was thought that the escape plot had been an Anglo-Dutch affair and that the British had preceded their colleagues and successfully escaped.

Best and Harvey were not caught, as they had not left the Castle in the first place. They had synchronised with the Dutch escape attempt to disappear and become 'ghosts.' They kept indoors at all time, hiding during roll-calls. The advantage of being a 'ghost' meant that when it came to escaping they, or others, would not be missed at roll-call, giving the escapee more time to get away. The Dutch had used dummies, the British used Harvey and Best.

Life as a 'ghost' was not that easy. At all roll-calls they hid, but eventually came into the courtyard, when it was thought safe. However, walks to the park were considered too dangerous. They would help with any escape plans, as they could.

RIGHT: Lieutenant. Michael Harvey, RN, one of the Colditz ghosts.

OFLAG V B 272

ABOVE: Cans of foods discovered from prisoners escape tunnels. Old tins are still being discovered at the castle. In 1997 a substantial collection such as these were found.

LEFT: Jack Best, one of the 'Colditz Ghosts' and was along with Bill Goldfinch, one of the constructors of the Colditz Glider.

Jack Best had an opportunity to take part in Mike Sinclair's incredible escape bid. Sinclair had noticed that there was a delay of one minute between darkness descending and the search lights put on. This made it difficult for the sentry in the machine gun tower to see, and he would join his colleagues while awaiting to be relieved by the night sentries. Within these sixty seconds, Best and Sinclair were to be propelled out of a British quarters window, drop thirty feet by rope, run across the west terrace past the German guard house, descend forty feet by rope to a garden area, run thirty feet across the garden, cut through barbed wire, and descend fifty foot down a precipice into the town. The prisoners' orchestra were to play at the start of the operation. Best and Sinclair practiced, becoming tremendously agile, and on the day, 19 January 1944, they managed to escape, although Sinclair almost knocked himself out, and a spike cut through Best's hand. Both had their clothes cut to pieces by the barbed wire, but they repaired these with the needle and thread Best had brought along. Elated at their freedom they made their way towards Holland, posing as Flemish workers. The alarm went off in Colditz, but action was delayed by a catapult aimed at the main lamp in the courtyard, fusing all the lights.

However, by their fourth day on the run, their rations had been used and although near their destination, they were picked up at the frontier town of Rheine. Best thought that one of the reasons he was spotted was because he was dark, when most Germans were fair, and also because he was so white from being a 'ghost.' Although both were sent back to Colditz, Best managed to do three weeks solitary as 'Barnes.'

Door to potato cellar.

Airey Neave

Airey Neave in the uniform of a Gefreiter (lance corporal). This picture was taken in the Kommandant's headquarters after his first unsuccessful attempt at escape through the main gate. The tunic and forage caps were of Polish origin and Neave used paints from the theatrical department to change the colour from khaki into German field grey. Unfortunately for Neave, under the arch lights used at night the colour changed from field grey to bright emerald. He was sentenced to 28 days solitary confinement, but four months later, he had a new plan. This time he reasoned that by impersonating German officers, they would less likely be challenged by the ordinary soldier, particularly within such familiar surroundings. Neave and Luteijn were selected by Pat Reid, the escape officer, to make the first attempt. The Dutch supplied the most vital part of the bogus uniform, pre-war Dutch Home Army great coats, which with slight alterations, could be made to appear identical to the coats worn by German officers. Although blue-green in colour, in the light of the arch-lamp at night, they appeared field-grey.

While Pat Reid was serving a period of solitary confinement, he studied the Saalhaus opposite which housed the theatre on the third floor. It occurred to him that the stage on which the prisoners performed their shows, might extend over German

RIGHT: Airey Neave as a POW at Spangenburg.

154

OFLAG IX A 1198

controlled territory. If this was so, then it might be possible to gain access to the corridor which joined the Saalhaus to the guardhouse.

They escaped through a hole under the stage. Neave took the rank of Oberleutnant and called himself Schwartz. The gold star epaulettes which denoted his rank, were carved from wood and painted gold. So by the night of 5 January 1942, they had the uniforms, documentation, civilian clothes and route maps to Switzerland. They escaped via passing a sentry, and Luteijn, in common with many Dutch, spoke excellent German, reprimanded the soldier for not saluting correctly. This bravado worked and they were soon at the castle walls where they climbed the wall and changed to civilian clothes.

Neave arrived at Leipzig on the morning of 6 January 1942. While waiting for a train Neave and Dutchman Luteijn ate chocolate brought to the POWs from the Red Cross. This attracted unwanted attention from the civilian population, because of its scarcity. They then walked the streets of Leipzig and decided to go to the cinema to kill time. Catching a train to Stockach, a village near the Swiss border, they crept across to Ramsen, a Swiss village, just 72 hours after their escape. Neave was the first Briton to successfully escape from Colditz. Meanwhile, Hyde-Thomson and

RIGHT: Airey Neave dressed as a German Corporal, photographed by the Germans after his first escape attempt.

the Dutchman, Donkers, who also escaped later, were caught. The two Dutch dummies, Max and Mortiz, which concealed the first two departures at the time of roll-call, did not conceal the later two. When Neave and Luteijn, posing as itinerant Dutch electrical workers were questioned by a suspicious booking office official, they narrowly escaped recapture. So when the latter two also presented themselves as Dutch workers, at Ulm, they were immediately arrested and sent back to Colditz.

On arriving at Switzerland, Luteijn and Neave were split-up and Neave was put with Captain Hugh Woollatt, of the Lancashire Fusiliers. Neave sent a postcard of Swiss girls in traditional dress to the Kommandant of Colditz, saying that he had arrived safely and hoping that he wouldn't be sent to the divisional front on his account. When awaiting to leave the run down hotel, near lake Geneva they were obliged to register, Neave wrote 'Oscar Wilde' and Woollatt called himself 'Herr Albert Hall'. The following morning they were escorted by two uniformed Swiss police and taken out of Geneva in a car to a cemetery which separated the two countries. They were this time to travel through Vichy France as Czech refugees and try to reach Marseilles, in the then Unoccupied French Zone. Once over the border, they were assisted by members of the French resistance. The first to meet them was a former employee of the London Ritz. They were taken to his

LEFT: Entrance to one of the cellars. Above is a solitary confinement cell, into which unsuccessful escapees would be holed-up in after recapture.

home and given a hearty breakfast. From there, they were escorted by a young girl who asked if, when they safely reached Britain, they could confirm their arrival via the BBC, as everyone listened to the station to hear the news. They made it down to Marseilles and then crossed the border into neutral Spain, via Perpignan. From there, they travelled down through Spain to Gibraltar and back to the UK via the Clyde in May 1942.

Sadly, Woollatt was later killed in Normandy in July 1944. But he was not the only one of the escapees who died later in the war. Among the eleven British and Empire Colditz escapees, Flight-Lieutenant H.N. Fowler, M.C. RAF who escaped through the German Sergeant-major's office, reaching Switzerland in 1942, was killed whilst flying two years later. Major R.B. Littledale D.S.O. who escaped along with Pat Reid was killed in action in Normandy in August 1944. Airey Neave, who became a Conservative MP for Abingdon for nearly 26 years, was himself killed in a car bomb by the IRA in 1979. He was opposition spokesman on Northern Ireland.

RIGHT: This a reconstruction by the photographer Lange of how Neave and Luteijn and then later Hyde-Thomson and Donkers escaped. After each escape, the hole was re-sealed by the POWs, as it was hoped that this route could be used again.

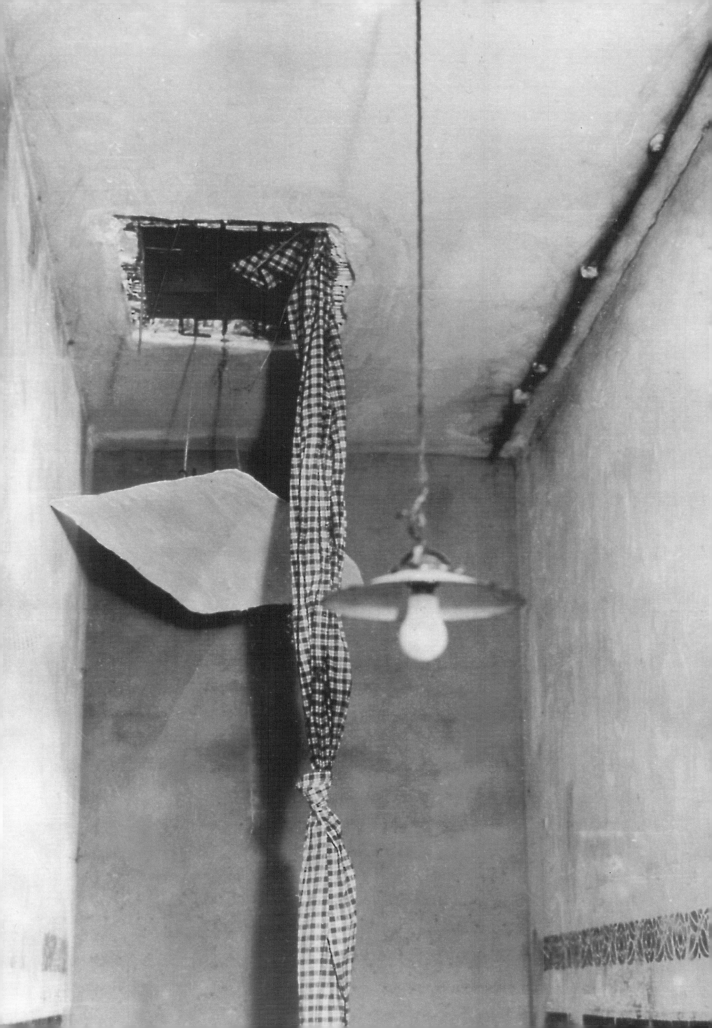

Escape to Sweden

Soon after Neave's escape, Squadron-Leader Brian Paddon also escaped, this time via Sweden. He had been sent to Thorn in Posen for a court-marshal. Originally he had escaped from hospital along with four others but was recaptured and sent for trial. He then had escaped again via a toilet window. Having gained passage on a boat, he sailed to neutral Sweden and from there to England.

Pat Reid

Pat Reid's escape on 14 October 1942, with three other British Officers is one of Colditz's classics. His basic idea was to try to enter the tall Kommandantur building on the south side of the German part of the castle. Once there, he hoped that it would be possible to climb down on a rope from the outer windows into the moat. He then intended to follow Neave's route from nine month's before.

On the morning of the 15 October 1942, Major R. B. Littledale, Lieutenant-Commander W. E. Stephens, Flight Lieutenant H. D. Wardle along with Captain Reid were found to be missing.

LEFT: **View from a cell window.**

The escape completely puzzled the Germans. The mystery was only revealed to security officer Reinhold Eggers when he was released from Soviet detention in 1956 and he read Reid's account in his book *The Colditz Story*.

They had, from the corner of the prisoners' yard, gained access to the kitchens, via a broken window. Once inside, the four, along with squadron leader McColm in a supportive role, cleared all traces of their entry and went to the second floor and climbed through the windows overlooking the German yard. A window bar had already been loosened and they climbed through. From here, they had to negotiate directly across the path of a patrolling sentry. Douglas Bader was watching and he had arranged for music to be played every time that it was safe to cross. This didn't quite work as planned and the escapees had to run across while the sentry's back was turned. Then they ran across the front of the Kommandantur's terrace to a pit by the doorway. From there they went down into a cellar. They worked their way under the building and found an air vent only nine inches by three foot, leading to outside, but the only way they could squeeze through was by taking off all of their clothes and climbing out backwards. Reid was the first to try and his colleague Wardle passed through all of his clothes and suitcase. Eventually all four managed to escape and safely reached Switzerland.

ABOVE: The west terrace in winter, showing spot lights and sentry with rifle.
OVERLEAF: Top left to right: Lieut Allan, F/Lieut. Middleton, F/Lieut H. Wardle, T.Elliott, Padre Heard, Lieut P. Storie-Pugh, Padre Hobling, Lieut G. Wardle, Captain K. Lockwood. Middle row; Padre Platt, Lieut/Col German, Captain H. A. V. Elliott, Captain R. R. F. T. Barry. Front row; Lieut H. Barton, Captain P. R. Reid (Escape First Officer), Captain R. H. Howe (Second Escape Officer).

ABOVE: The Kommandantur.

LEFT: Entrance to the cellar under the Kommandantur. It was through here that Pat Reid escaped, climbing through an air vent at the end.

OVERLEAF: The Kommandantur viewed from the entrance.

Liberation

This occurred on 16 April 1945, when the 9th Armoured division of the US army came from the west to meet other allied armies and liberated 300 allied POWs. On the following Tuesday, they were allowed to leave the prison and go to the town at Colditz, but warned not to wander to the surrounding countryside. Two Frenchmen who ignored this order, were recaptured by the Germans, disappeared and never seen again.

The nearby cities of Leipzig and Dresden were in ruins because of allied bombing. Between 14-16 February three bombing raids by RAF and the USAF left an estimated 100,000 - 300,000 dead.

The last Kommandant of Colditz from May 1943 was Colonel Prawitt, shown left, who was given a safe conduct letter by senior British Officer Colonel Tod, Brigadier Davies and Lieutenant Colonel Duke. For a time after the war the town was divided into two across the River Mulde, with the Americans controlling one half and the Russians, the other. Townspeople needed a passport to cross the two halves. The Americans later withdrew to a pre-agreed demarcation line, as the town was in the Soviet sector.

Jam-Alc

Through their illegal radios the prisoners knew that the war was drawing to a close, and as allied victory was assured, they put to one side thoughts of escape. Rations were becoming poorer and they could not make wine as they had earlier in the war. Also they would no longer be able to help the war effort because if they were caught by the retreating Germans they were likely to be shot.

While waiting to be rescued, Pat Fergusson and George Drew remember brewing an illicit alcoholic substance called Jam-Alc, made from German ration jam. The still in which it was made was produced using purloined pipes and medical plaster. Not surprisingly, it apparently tasted awful.

Surrender

German sentries were kept for the sake of appearances. On Saturday 14 April, with the Americans shelling the town and flying a reconnaissance plane overhead, Colonel Tod was called to Kommandant Prawitt's office. He was told that the British were to be moved out of the castle and towards the east as orders had come from Dresden. Tod refused, knowing that the SS were themselves under attack and could not deal with three hundred British and a further thousand Frenchmen. In the middle of a battle they could not even spare the opportunity to come and shoot them all.

'The British refuse to move,' Tod said. 'You will have to turn them out with a bayonet and the British will fight. This is not mutiny. It is self-defence. You are sending them to their deaths. Tell Dresden we shall not move.'

The Kommandant reported back to Dresden saying 'I cannot move the prisoners without shooting them and they will then resist. Their Commander will disclaim mutiny on grounds of self-defence. Will you take the responsibility if I use my weapons and prisoners are killed?'
'No!' was shouted down the 'phone.
'Neither will I!' replied the Kommandant and banged down the receiver.

A few shells came crashing into the castle, but none of the prisoners were hurt although Douglas Bader was knocked off his tin legs.

In the early afternoon Colonel Tod again met with the Kommandant, who had a proposal. He would surrender on two conditions: No white flags were to be displayed, nor any national flags displayed as the some of the SS were still in the town. German sentries were to remain at their posts and that he, Oberst Prawitt, would not be handed over to the Russians.

The Colonel refused to give any guarantees. Instead he proposed an alternative plan which was he would like the keys to the armoury, but agreed he would not give any outward signs that the prison had changed hands and surrendered, thereby not provoking any of the SS who may still be in the town. He would also ensure that the Kommandant was treated with justice. The risk from the SS was receding, but there was a danger that the Americans, not knowing who was in the Castle, might blow it up. The odd shell that had entered the castle were, he considered, 'off target.' All through the night of the 14th to 15th the battle for Colditz town continued and the electrical supply was cut. Keith Milne had spotted the American tanks through his telescope. On the following day, Sunday 15 April, American shell fire was at its heaviest and still the castle was not hit. Colonel Shaughnessy had seen one of the prisoners display a red white and blue flag, and knew that this was the castle where the POWs were being held so they continued their attack elsewhere.

By 16 April, a task force comprising of the 69th Infantry division and 9th armoured Division, which was part of the US First Army, entered the gates of Colditz and the prisoners were free.

The Colditz Glider

Never has an escape plan from a prisoner-of-war camp been incredible as that of the glider constructed secretly in Colditz.

By autumn 1944, its construction was underway. It was a British idea and the officers involved in its creation were Flight Lieutenant Bill Goldfinch, Jack Best, Lieutenant Tony Rolt of the Rifle Brigade and Captain David Walker of the Black Watch and Lieutenant Geoff 'Stooge' Wardle, RN.

Goldfinch, a professional draftsman, before the war, produced the designs, Rolt established an elaborate early warning system. Walker acquired the materials and Best, a versatile craftsman, along with Goldfinch, supervised the planes construction. It was built in the empty attic above the prisoners chapel and behind false walls which were themselves made out of plastered canvas and covered frames. Much of the walls material was made from debris left over from the French tunnel project, so when it dried it perfectly matched the surrounding walls, and so was undiscovered during the nine months of the glider's construction. The attic overlooked the roof of an adjoining building which was to be used as a launching pad as the gilder was to be catapulted clear of the castle.

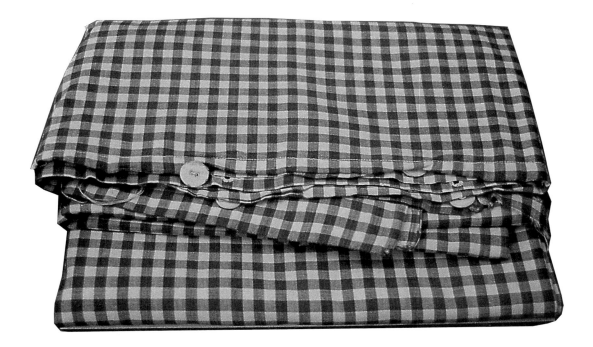

ABOVE: The checked cloth was used to cover the fuselage of the glider.

TOP: The glider at the end of the war

Shortly after the war, the original glider was broken up and used as firewood.
The picture above is the remade copy of the glider using the same materials
and specifications. It was taken at the Imperial War Museum, London.

On the planned day of the launch, they were to break through the attic wall and carry out the fuselage and the sixteen foot wing span was to be assembled on the roof on a trolley which was to be attached by pulleys. It was then to be dropped 60 foot through the castle floors, which was to provide enough thrust to launch the two seater along the 60 foot ramp and fly a distance of 900 foot. Called the 'Colditz Cock' it was never put to the test because it was finished in January 1945, and by then they had heard via illicit radio that the war would be soon over and they would be liberated. Also the Germans were now shooting escapees.

When the film-makers Windfall, produced a documentary, 55 years later for Channel 4, they re-made the gilder using original designs and materials, and they proved that the glider would have flown as intended.

The Colditz Phenomenon

Colditz was like no other POW camp and its extraordinary escapes and tales have produced great media interest. Soon after the war and publication of Pat Reid's book *The Colditz Story*, the British film by the same name made by Ivan Foxwell came out in 1955. Staring John Mills as Pat Reid it retold much of the Colditz story, but changed the names of other POWs. Pat Reid, an engineer before the war, also acted as advisor on the film and on the BBC Television series in the 1970s. It was his writings that started the huge interest in Colditz.

Over seventy books have been published and several recent television documentaries have been broadcast. Written accounts have come from the British, Dutch, French and the Germans.

In Germany, however, Colditz is far less well known. This is partly because during the time of the GDR regime, the Communists refused to acknowledge Oflag IVC as 'Capitalist' officers had been stationed there. The only official English-language guide made no mention of the camp. However since reunification tourists have been a more positively encouraged.

RIGHT: The Colditz glider story inspired this children's toy, from the 1970s.

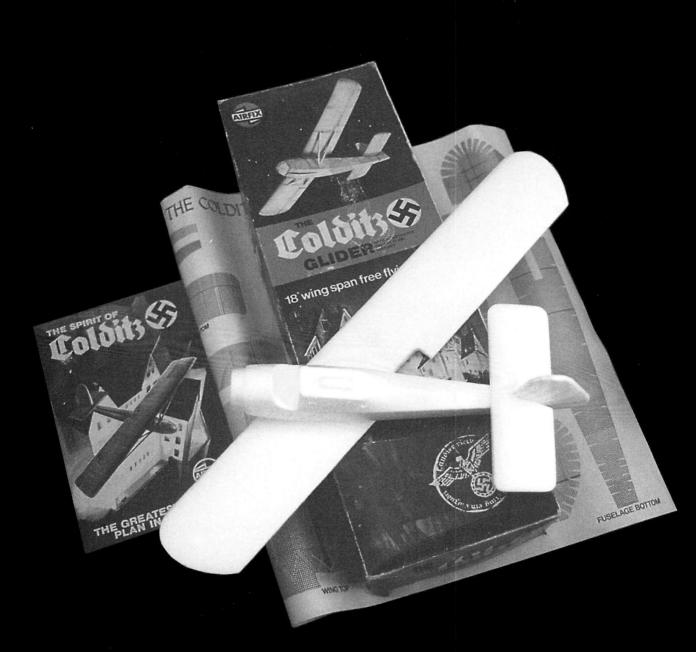

FURTHER READING

The Colditz Story
By Pat Reid, M.B.E., M.C.

The Latter Days at Colditz
By Pat Reid, M.B.E., M.C.

Colditz: The German Story
By Reinhold Eggers

Escape from Colditz: 16 First Hand Accounts
Reinhold Eggers

They Have Their Exits
Airey Neave

www.colditz-4c.com

IMPERIAL WAR MUSEUM PICTURE CREDITS
Page 14&15: HU86548, 18&19: HU20272, 22: HU20293,
23: HU20291, 32&33: HU20287, 36: HU20288, 40: HU86543,
41: HU865440, 42: HU86535, 43: HU58539, 44: HU60903,
45: HU58537, 46: HU86533, 47: HU86534, 48: HU49539,
49: HU49538, 58: HU86545, 64: HU51018, 69: HU86536,
70: HU51017, 72&73: IW49534, 74: HU41545, 78&79: HU49543
81: HU86539, 85: HU86537, 86: HU86568, 90: HU4225,
92: HU41544, 94&95: HU49546, 96: IW41548, 104: HU86542,
109: HU44226, 116&117: HU20282, 120&121: HU4228,
123: IW49544, 124: 41546, 132: HU54526, 134: HU86569,
142: IW76200, 145: HU76199, 149: HU86544, 150: HU86538,
155: HU86547,156: HU41547, 161: HU49533, 165:HU86541,
166&167: HU54527, 172: HU86570.

Page 8&9 and Front cover, copyright David Ray, 179: US National
Archives all other pictures copyright Keith Pointing